Radical Life Extension

Additional Publications from Michael Ten

This is not the first book by Michael Ten. Here are two other books authored by me.

Attempt to Utilize Cryonics (First Edition): Reasons Why Utilizing Human Cryopreservation Is Ultimately Desirable

Outlaw Psychiatric Slavery (First Edition): Reasons for Outlawing Civil Commitment and the Insanity Defense

Additional Publications from Scott Everhart

This is the first book published by Scott Everhart.

Radical Life Extension

Psychological, Metaphysical,
and Political Implications

Michael Ten

Scott Everhart

Radical Life Extension

Psychological, Metaphysical, and Political Implications

ISBN-13: 978-1514292327

ISBN-10: 1514292327

Websites: MichaelTen.com and ScottEverhart.com

Twitter: @iMichaelTen or @iScottEverhart

Facebook: Facebook.com/tenmichael or Facebook.com/aScottEverhart

Email: hello@MichaelTen.com or hello@ScottEverhart.com

Acknowledgements and Dedications

I appreciate all those who have guided me in authentically beneficial ways and those who have motivated me to create more goodness and peace on Earth.

I appreciate all family, friends, and others that have helped me in many various ways.

I also want to specifically thank Sef Ramos for helping me to proof and polish this book, and Monica Hernandez for illustrating the wonderful cover art.

I dedicate this book to all humans who attempt to live lives of authentic decency.

Table of Contents

Preface

The message of this book is ultimately fairly simple. Individually and collectively we can think more clearly about human aging, and about deaths resulting from natural aging and suicides. That is, currently most individuals think about human aging, death and dying in certain ways and therefore behave in certain ways in relation to those ideas; the same goes for suicide. In this book I am suggesting that we should think differently about biological aging, dying, death and suicide, so that we behave differently. The ways in which we collectively behave in relation to our thoughts about biological aging, dying, death and suicide can have profound implications for humanity.

We may be able to defeat aging. That is, although it is currently science fiction, in the perhaps not too distant future (maybe twenty to fifty years) we as humans might be able to utilize biomedical technologies to stop and reverse human aging. I will provide evidence of the credibility of this statement in the following sections of this book. If developed, radical life extension technologies will result in radical changes for us humans here on Earth. These could be a mix of positive, negative and neutral effects. The mere possibility of defeating aging might seem farfetched right now, but please consider the contents of this short book and do your own research if needed in order to realize how far we have already advanced and developed biomedical technologies and how the accelerating pace of change may enable us to soon achieve what not long ago more easily seemed to be an impossibility. To not support further development of these sorts of now fictional technologies is to be in a pro-aging mindset. To embrace this mindset (that it is undesirable to try and utilize science and biomedical technologies to defeat aging) and to actively resist changing it despite contradictory evidence may be not much different than embracing death, and can even potentially be considered a form of slow suicide. To not think of human biological aging and the resulting deaths from aging as tragic is like being willing to not think of deaths from communicable and non-communicable diseases as tragic. Deaths from suicides are also tragic.

Our attitudes about suicide may affect our attitudes about radical life extension technologies. Support for developing radical life extension technologies may increase if suicides are seen as a the moral and ethical issue that they are, rather than being medicalized to the point of great numbers of individuals, societies and governments using medical justifications on a massive scale to utilize psychiatric force, coercion and confinement daily on thousands of adults who feel motivated to utilize suicide but have not broken any actual laws. It will be good if we can reduce suicides to zero on Earth. However coercion and force are not the route to successfully seeing this happen. Persuasion, reason, and kindness are.

By reading this book I hope that you will become aware (or more aware) of some important issues that if thought about clearly can result in a desire to potentially end human aging, one of the greatest human tragedies that has ever existed, if not the greatest.

Introduction

This book is about psychological, metaphysical and political implications of radical life extension technologies. Ultimately this book is meant to further the research related radical life extension technologies. This is a relatively short book. I will also cover cryonics some in this book. Cryonics relates to radical life extension in that cryonic technologies (freezing humans after legal death) may enable individuals to eventually utilize life extension technologies that do not currently exist.

Aging is the largest humanitarian crisis on Earth in terms of sheer numbers of humans who die from it. In the book *Ending Aging: The Rejuvenation Breakthroughs That Could Reverse Human Aging in Our Lifetime*, Aubrey de Grey and Michael Rae write about a pro-aging trance that many individuals are stuck in. This book is meant to help awaken some away from the pro-aging trance and to hopefully help increase the amount of support and recognition that radical life extension and cryonics technologies have.

I have been interested in life extension technologies since about 2009. Since that time I have spoken with many individuals who are not for defeating aging. They may come around eventually and no longer have a pro aging mindset at some point. Life extension for humans has happened over the last few thousand years. It has happened even in the last one hundred years. The amount of gains in the average life span that can be achieved through current technological and medical approaches is diminishing rapidly. Without significantly different approaches, the average human lifespan will likely stop increasing at some point. Even now it is just increasing quite slowly, maybe at about one year every decade. Radical life extension differs from the non-radical life extension technologies that humanity has been slowly utilizing over the last few thousand years in that radical life extension technologies may enable humans to live indefinitely. If radical life extensions are developed, humans who utilize them could still die from accidents and so forth, just simply not diseases caused by bodily aging. This might sound farfetched and unrealistic. This book is not about the details of biological mechanisms and engineering strategies that might enable humans to utilize radical life extension. If you are curious about how it might actually work bio-medically, read the book *Ending Aging*, or follow the work of Aubrey de Grey (who earned a doctorate degree from Cambridge), Human Longevity Inc. (co-founded by Craig Venter who helped sequence the first human genome), California Life Company (funded by Google) or David Sinclair (Harvard affiliated biologist).

Since 2009 many new developments have taken place. Human Longevity Inc. is a new business that has formed. Peter Diamandis, when being interviewed by Seth Green, notes something about attempting to have 100 become the new 60 with this new venture. [1] Craig Venter, an eminent biologist, has co-founded this venture with Peter Diamandis.

Some of the contents of this short book might be a bit controversial. However, this book is about issues related to extending life and reducing or postponing deaths, and the because of the intimate nature of what life and death is for humans, unless one censors oneself, controversy may be hard to avoid. I am relatively libertarian in my views. I think that suicide should be respected a civil and human right; that is death control (deciding when one dies and ceases one's own life) should be just as legal as birth control (deciding when one's body creates life). Just as outlawing birth control leads to negative unintended consequences, outlawing death control has also lead to negative unintended consequences. That is a subject for another book for the most part. However, talking about death control and birth control are both relevant when discussing radical life extension from philosophical, metaphysical, psychological and political perspectives.

One key suggestion I want to make in this short book is that not supporting radical life extension research may not be far from accepting a slow suicide. I will cover this idea in this book some. Of course, just as I support the right for adults to engage in suicide, I also support the right of adults to not support radical life extension research and cryonics utilization. I support this right even though I believe it to be a poor choice.

Radical life extension may change how humans experience life dramatically. Currently, humans grow old and die. There are many reasons why humans die. Not all deaths are due to aging of course. However, of all the different causes of death, aging kills the most. If we are able to miraculously eliminate just one cause of death, if we want to make the most difference, to stop the most deaths, then we should pick aging as the one cause of death to eliminate.

Psychological Considerations

One interesting thing that I have noticed when talking to different individuals about the topic of radical life extension technologies is that they might say that they would theoretically be interested in living to be maybe around 400 years with the body of a 20 something year old, but then they might want to stop living at some point. In the context of radical life extension, individuals more often will agree that suicide should be respected as a right if radical life extension technologies do exist.

Suicide is currently effectively illegal. The way proposed therapies to defeat aging might work is sort of a maintenance approach, at least the ones that the doctor Aubrey de Grey has proposed. So, if one does want to die after 400 years, if these therapies are successfully created, all that one would have to do is to stop receiving the therapies.

Psychiatrist Thomas Szasz's book, *Fatal Freedom: The Ethics and Politics of Suicide,* impacted me significantly. It has lead me to ask in my own mind questions that I otherwise might not have asked. If one has a potentially lethal cancer but rejects treatment, they will die. Is this a form of suicide? If one refuses food and starves to death, is that not a form of suicide? If one requires insulin due to diabetes but intentionally does not take the required insulin and then dies, is that not a form of suicide? What about if someone requires kidney dialysis but then stops the kidney dialysis and then dies; is that not a form of suicide?

No one that I know of with any credibility claims that defeating aging is inevitable and certain, but simply that it is a potential based on where biomedical technology is today and where it might be able to be in the future. So if one (who is aware of the potential existence of technologies that may be able to dramatically increase the average human life span) does not advocate for increasing funding towards biomedical gerontological research that may help to defeat aging, is that not at least potentially a form of suicide? Furthermore, if radical life extension technologies are developed, if one does not receive them, would that not be a form of suicide? This comes back to the issue of the feasibility of defeating aging.

Psychological Considerations, Radical Life Extension and Death Control

Personally, if I knew suicide was not effectively illegal I would support research related to radical life extension technologies even more than I do already.

I think that more individuals would support research related to radical life extension technologies if death were definitely a relatively easy option to choose after 100 or 200 or more years of living. A probably greater problem towards furthering radical life extension research is simply a lack of awareness that these technologies might be able to exist in the next twenty to thirty years.

Suicide is at least somewhat taboo. Most individuals have an aversion to thinking about suicide. Yet, radical life extension, when thinking about living past 100 or 500 years, brings up thoughts related to death. Thoughts and questions that might pass through one's mind when thinking about radical life extension might include some of the following. What if I want to die after 400 (or any number of years past today's life expectancies) years? Will I want to live past 80? God wants me to be in Heaven and not interfere with his plan for my natural death.

Radical Life Extension

There are an infinite number of potential objections to radical life extension and cryonics technologies. I tend to be quite libertarian about certain things. Death is one of those things. I support free access to birth control for adults and some minors. Birth control enables individuals to choose when they create life. Why should adults not also be able to utilize death control methods without interference from governments (police officers and so forth) and other authorized entities (like hospitals, social workers and psychiatrists)? I support adults' rights to utilize birth control and death control. This does not mean that suicide is necessarily a moral decision, but just that adults should have the right to make the decision if they choose to and cannot be peacefully and non-coercively persuaded not to. Issues related to death and suicide relate to radical life extension technologies in the sense that if we think more clearly about death, from aging and other means, then we might more clearly think about life and the potential to extend it significantly.

Metaphysical and Theological Considerations

It is easy to think that aging and death is the natural order of life on Earth. All humans are meant to die from aging, right? Maybe or maybe not. It can be easy to accept the status quo. This book is not meant to be primarily about theology. However, death from aging leads to a potential afterlife. This section is about metaphysical and theological considerations with respect to aging, dying, and the potential of radical life extension technologies.

Most humans accept the existence of an afterlife. Biological disease and pathology have been a normal part of the human experience since the dawn of humanity. Yet, we still attempt to defeat diseases and pathologies through antibiotics, vaccines, antivirals, antifungals and all sorts of other drugs and treatments. Humans have attempted to heal broken bones so that they are functional again since before written history. Since the dawn of modern humanity (as a species), the idea that disease and pathology are normal (normal in the sense that they are natural and therefore nothing should be done to stop them) for the most part has not been accepted.

If one is an atheist then attempting to develop radical life extension technologies might not matter. There are many types of atheists. There is no atheist Pope so there is no one official atheist metaphysical doctrine. An atheist might reason that it is enjoyable to live, and since there is no after life, he or she might as well try to live as long as possible. Therefore, they might choose to help promote and further research related to radical life extension. A different atheist might decide that life is not significantly enjoyable nor worth living and therefore be apathetic to or against attempting to develop radical life extension technologies. Agnostics could have similar examples.

A theist could reason that God wants us to enjoy life and health for as long as possible, and to live life on Earth in ways that help to reduce tragedies on Earth in order to help enable Earth to be more like it might be in Heaven. And since infirmity and dying from biological aging are part of what helps to have this Earth seem less Heaven like, then from a theological and metaphysical perspective, it is justifiable and even desirable to try and defeat aging and develop radical life extension technologies if possible.

Another theist of the same or different religion might reason that aging is natural, and to try to defeat it is to try to usurp the power of God, which is wrong. Therefore, we should not attempt to defeat aging, even if it might be possible. However, can they easily justify as to why we should not attempt to defeat aging if there is even a remote possibility of potentially doing so, but then at the same time try to defeat diseases like infections and so forth simply so that we can becoming infirm after a few gained decades and then die from aging?

There are an infinite number of potentially unique reasons why an agnostic, theist, or atheist might be for or against attempting to defeat aging. Rather than write a book of rebuttals, my whole goal is to enable you to more clearly think about aging and death so you can ask yourself questions that you might not otherwise ask and thereby be able to move your mind to a spot where you are motivated to help defeat one of the largest if not the largest killer of humans in our entire existence, aging, however you might realistically be able to.

A significant number of humans, collectively and individually, have attempted to stop diseases like small pox, malaria, leprosy and so forth. Do we as humans have a tendency to just label diseases as metaphysically natural and then not bother to try and remedy them? For the most part, not really. Why in our minds should we treat biological aging (which also causes death) any different than other diseases and pathologies? Just because up until recently it was a lot easier to see defeating aging as an impossibility?

Aging is different from other death causing phenomenon in that before the last few decades the chances of humans being able to stop or reverse biological aging has been slim to none. With technologies like genome sequencing, genetic engineering, tissue engineering, and regenerative medicine all emerging, it is seems hard to deny that humans at least might be able to stop, reverse, and defeat aging. Again, this book is not meant to be about the detailed technical aspects of how aging might be defeated. For that, again, please read the book *Ending Aging*, look up Aubrey de Grey on YouTube (there are interviews, TED Talks, and more), look on Human Longevity Incorporated's website, or Methuselah Foundation's website, or do your own research in a different fashion. Information is now fairly easy to find on how defeating aging might happen using biomedical technologies.

Because of theology, some individuals believe that it is wrong to receive a blood transfusion or vaccine. As long as it is an adult who dies because of their own beliefs and not a child, I take a libertarian perspective on this even though I disagree with dying this way as being a decent or likely moral life choice. I support the rights of adults to die from old age or suicide. I just hope that more individuals consider all current potentialities fully before resigning oneself to any one way of dying.

Theologies and spiritualities can be utilized to justify violence. Theologies and spiritualities (or the absence of them) can be used to justify anything. This is not to imply that all justifications are intelligent, sensible or moral. Just because some political or ideological position has a spiritual or theological justification does not make it true, decent, right, or moral.

How much have you ever questioned your implicit and explicit thoughts about aging and death? Think for yourself. Utilize critical thinking. Question what you are told or recommended to believe. It is possible to utilize theologies to justify not attempting to defeat aging. It is also possible to utilize theological lines of reasoning to justifying why societies should attempt to defeat aging.

Political Implications

There are a variety of political implications that relate to radical life extension research and also the technologies once (or if) they are successfully developed. For this section I must note that the aforementioned book *Ending Aging* talks about what is referred to as strategies for engineered negligible senescence (SENS), see the website for SENS Foundation or read the book *Ending Aging* for more detailed information than is needed here. SENS is a theoretically technological road map about how scientists and researches might go about defeating aging and developing radical life extension technologies. The following is how politics and radical life extension collide and how politics can potentially help to further the development of radical life extension technologies.

Politics Affecting Support for Radical Life Extension Research

Who would want to live a thousand years if death is not an option? In theory of course, if one lives to be five hundred years of age, one could then stop taking the therapies that prevent death and keep one biologically healthy and vigorous. That presumes maintenance therapies are required every few years or decades to keep aging away. What if the therapies are not ongoing? What if they can be administered over the course of a year and then you never need them again? What other option would one have in order to stop living other than proactive (rather than passive) suicide? Without proactive suicide, there would be no other option of dying other than patience and risk taking; if biological radical life extension technologies are developed, one can still die from accidental bodily trauma.

For a moment let's presume SENS technologies are successfully developed in twenty years. In this imaginary scenario, suppose some individuals live to be four hundred years of age (or however now impossibly long) and then do not feel like living anymore. In this scenario, should an individual be effectively forced to then die of old age after living four hundred years? Of course not. One could make a theological argument as to why one should not engage in suicide after four hundred years. Theology can be used to justify anything, including violence. Theology has been used as a justification for murdering heretics and supposed witches in the past. Theological justifications do not turn morally deficient political positions into morally sufficient political positions.

I am not implying that one should not have a faith or theology, but simply that one's theology should not be used as a justification to politically oppress others. In this currently fictional scenario, if current laws were applied, the oppressed individual would be the 400 year old who wants to die and would have to risk potential psychiatric confinement for attempting to actively engage in suicide, rather than passively engaging in suicide by no longer accepting life extending therapies.

Currently, if nothing changes, if someone is able to live to be four hundred years of age, and then decides that they no longer want to live, if they become "a danger to self", then they can be effectively imprisoned. This is science fiction right now, but this potential scenario might happen at some point in the future if current laws are not changed. At what age then should an otherwise healthy adult have the right to engage in suicide? Eighteen? One hundred? Four hundred? Never?

The purpose of this book is not to be primarily about suicide. However, this book is inherently about life and death. This book is meant to further the goals of radical life extension research. If suicide were medicalized less, and force would not be used on adults who decide to actively engage in suicide, then maybe more individuals might actively support political action to provide government funding for research that might help to defeat aging.

Government funding has been utilized for all sorts of amazing projects related to travel in outer space and nuclear research. Nuclear research was unimaginable three hundred years ago. Technologies enabling human flight did not exist barely more than one hundred years ago. Before technologies for flying were invented, many individuals thought flying was an impossibility. Who would have thought it possible for humans to fly astronauts to the moon and back on rockets three hundred years ago, or even just one hundred years ago?

It does not matter how taboo suicide might be. The politics of suicide relate to the politics of radical life extension research and funding. I support radical life extension research. I support efforts to reduce suicides to the point of none occurring. When viewed from a multi-century perspective, prohibitions against suicide make less sense. Support for radical life extension research might increase, if the thought of being trapped on Earth for hundreds of years after being ready to leave is not a potential political or cognitive problem. Especially because of the current political climate related to suicide, I think that it is also important to reiterate that we should attempt to significantly reduce suicides through persuasion, kindness and reason rather than force, coercion and confinement. Using force, coercion and, confinement is probably counterproductive to the worthwhile goal of helping all humans to want to live on Earth, rather than having a significant number of us humans engaging in suicide every year.

Funding and Democratic Political Will

Funding for research related to radical life extension technologies should increase. Government funding has been used to fund different types of research for a decently long time now. Radical life extension is a technology that may eventually be developed for all citizens of Earth.

Lacking Access to Radical Life Extension Technologies

Currently, human cryopreservation is available to those who are relatively wealthy or plan ahead many years (by spreading out the funding cryonic preservation over the years through life insurance policies).

I think that it is a legitimate concern that radical life extension technologies might only be available to wealthy individuals if they are developed successfully.

Suppose radical life extension technologies are developed. What if they are easily affordable and all humans on Earth are given access to these technologies? What if individuals who do not want to utilize them are declared insane and incompetent; what if all humans are forced to receive radical life extension technologies so that they can live indefinitely? I think that that would be extremely unfortunate and a definite abuse of human rights. What should the limit of the states' power be?

If radical life extension technologies are developed, some have a concern that only wealthy individuals would be able to access them. This might be a valid concern. If economically possible, if these technologies are developed, then it would be most ethical and moral if governments help provide funding so that they are available to all individuals that want to receive them.

Collective Popular Political Will

I hope that politics can cease being a barrier to radical life extension research. Once more individuals become aware of the potential of radical life extension technologies and realize how far we have already developed as a species technologically and medically, then I think that a combination of government and private funding can help propel research to the next level that may help to defeat aging.

Cryonics (A Metaphorical Ambulance to the Future)

I want to take a bit of time to discuss cryonic technologies. Human cryopreservation is a relatively new technology that chills the human body to the point of it being cryogenically preserved after what is considered legal death occurs. This will make more sense in a moment. Both whole body cryopreservation and just neuropreservation occur. Alcor Life Extension Foundation is one of the main organizations that will actually implement cryonic technologies upon legal death for individuals. There are other cryonics organizations that exist.

I do not have a great deal to write about cryonics in this book. However, I think that it is important to note here what cryonics is, and that it can be a potential back up strategy for those that desire to see aging defeated here on Earth even if radical life extension technologies are not successfully developed within the next twenty to fifty or so years. I have written more about cryonics in the book *Attempt to Utilize Cryonics: Reasons Why Utilizing Human Cryopreservation Is Ultimately Desirable*. Those that utilize cryogenic preservation hope that medical technology will eventually become advanced enough to revive them from the cryopreserved state (and keep them alive in a healthy and vigorous state).

The cost of utilizing cryonic technologies should be reduced if technologically and economically possible. There are various ways in which individuals fund cryonic services. If one starts young, then it is possible to do it through life insurance policies.

Without funding through life insurance policies, full body cryopreservation can cost quite a significant amount of money. Although less expensive, neuropreservation can still cost a few thousand dollars. Research should be conducted so that the cost of cryopreservation services can plummet. If economically possible, public and private insurance organizations should offer funding for cryonics services upon legal death.

Conclusion

Radical life extension technologies are currently science fiction. They might not be fiction in twenty or more years. There is a possibility that human aging may be able to be defeated through biomedical technologies. With this book I hope to help accelerate progress that we as humans are able to make towards successfully developing radical life extension technologies. What is presented in this book are just a few of the angles by which the potential of radical life extension technologies can be examined from political, metaphysical, and psychological perspectives.

Right now, unless more and specific kinds of biomedical gerontological research occurs, then all humans currently living will die from aging (if not something else first) in the next 122 years. The oldest human ever (Jeanne Calment) lived to 122 years of age. Without technology changing and advancing dramatically here on Earth, the chances of humans living much over 122 are slim to none.

Moving radical life extension technologies from science fiction to nonfiction might be difficult to accomplish both technologically and bio-medically. However, there is no proof that it is an impossibility.

What I am proposing is that more individuals do what is possible to further the research related to radical life extension technologies and defeat aging. A combination and dramatic rise in funding from both private and public (government) sources has the potential to advance research related to radical life extension the most. This of course is presuming that the researchers that engage in research related to aspects of these potential technologies are ethical and competent in what they are doing.

Accelerating Progress

More individuals need to start being aware of the amazing possibilities that regenerative medicine and bio-medical gerontological research might be able to enable. More individuals need to stop having a pro-aging mindset.

I hope that by more closely examining some of the political, metaphysical and psychological aspects related to radical life extension, that it will motivate you to do what is realistically possible to help further research related to defeating aging. Many small actions by massive amounts of individuals can result in gargantuan positive changes.

Given the option, after living seventy-five years on Earth, who would want to have a body aged seventy-five years, versus one that only has the biological aging of a twenty-five year old? Who would rather be a little or a lot decrepit rather than rugged and vigorous?

I hope that through this book I can help to raise awareness for these potential lifesaving and life extending technologies. I also hope to help raise awareness about and increase the utilization of cryonic technologies that currently exist. With this book I hope to help significantly increase the amount of government and private funding that radical life extension research (and related supporting research) receives by helping to raise awareness about, and to help increase support for, the development of radical life extension technologies. I also hope to inspire some individuals to actually become involved in the scientific research and biology behind these potential technologies.

Courage is a core component of thinking clearly. It takes courage to embrace the potential of radical life extension technologies and cryonics. It takes courage to question one's own deeply held values, beliefs, and assumptions. We should do what we can to hasten the defeat of aging.

References

1. Peter Diamandis & Seth Green. Hammer Institute.
    YouTube. July 19, 2014. Start: 1 min 27 sec.
    (https://www.youtube.com/watch?v=dqYP4OHW2Go
    &feature=youtu.be&t=27m01s).
    Shortened: (http://goo.gl/FjcHh4).
    Cited: Introduction, 4th paragraph.

Book Recommendations

These are books that I have not written but that I believe are worth reading or listening to.

Ending Aging: The Rejuvenation Breakthroughs That Could Reverse Human Aging in Our Lifetime
by Aubrey de Grey and Michael Rae

Abundance: The Future Is Better Than You Think
by Peter H. Diamandis and Steven Kotler

The Art of Non-Conformity: Set Your Own Rules, Live the Life You Want, and Change the World
by Chris Guillebeau

The Art of Peace
by John Stevens and Morihei Ueshiba

Fatal Freedom: The Ethics and Politics of Suicide
by Thomas Szasz

Suicide Prohibition: The Shame of Medicine
by Thomas Szasz

Afterword

Thank you for reading this book. I hope that it has motivated you to think differently about death from human aging.

Please leave an honest review of this book where you are able to.

Additionally, please sign up for my mailing list so that you can stay up to date on when I release future books. You can sign up for the mailing list at www.MichaelTen.com/Subscribe or at www.DoNothingMedia.com/Suscribe or just visit my website at www.MichaelTen.com.

You can also subscribe to Scott Everhart's list at www.ScottEverhart.com/Subscribe or just visit his website at www.ScottEverhart.com.